Pray Unceasingly:
A Shorter Breviary
for Daily Use

*Sanctifying moments of peace in the
midst of your daily life.*

Compiled, Translated, and Edited by
Cameron M. Thompson, PsyD., MA
& Katie H. Thompson, MA

Published by

Marchese di Carabàs

an imprint of Acropolis Scholars, LLC

Copyright © 2020 Cameron M. Thompson

ISBN: 0692809708
ISBN-13: 978-0692809709

A Liturgy of the Hours simplified to integrate into modern
life using a traditional structure of passages of sacred
scripture and the ancient prayers of the Church.

CONTENTS

ACKNOWLEDGEMENTS

In honor of those who taught me to pray the liturgy of the people of God.

This work is dedicated to you, who in faithfully taking up the sanctification of the hours these prayers, are playing no small part in the restoration of this ancient Christian practice for the salvation of the world.

"In praying the liturgy of the hours the faithful are adoring God the Father *in spirit and in truth*; they should bear in mind that through this public worship and prayer they reach all humanity and can contribute, in no small way, to the salvation of the whole world."

– General Instruction on the Liturgy of the Hours in the Roman Catholic Church

"Pray Unceasingly."

(I Thessalonians 5:17)

INTRODUCTION

It is an ancient practice of the Church for individual Christians to set aside specific times of day to be sanctified by prayer. Indeed, this practice of offering formal prayer to God at particular times of day predates the Incarnation of Christ and reaches back to the ancient sacrifices and prayers established by the covenant with Moses. Even more than that, the sanctification of certain times of day harkens back to the very dawn of creation and honors the divine order God gave to the world when when he separated the light from the darkness and created the sun, moon, and stars to govern the passing of time.

Particular times of the day stand out as natural moments to be dedicated to God: upon rising just before dawn, morning praises as the day begins, midday prayers when the sun is at its highest, the evening sacrifice of thanksgiving and petition at dusk, completing the day at nightfall asking God to bless our sleep, and calling on God in prayer when we wake in the middle of the night. These times of prayer, more or less held in common across traditional Christian cultures throughout the world, became known in the West variously as *the work of God, the divine office,* and *the liturgy of the hours.* This ancient practice of ritual prayer was over time gradually forgotten in the West and all but fell out of practice except in secluded monasteries and among dedicated clergy. Nonetheless, this sacred practice, this *work of God,* is the inheritance of each and every Christian, regardless of whether they are cleric or lay, monastic or living in the world. Indeed, in recent years the Church has renewed the urgent call to each man and woman of good will to embrace their precious inheritance as sons and daughters of God and revive the practice of liturgical prayer at the key moments of the day.

It is nonetheless difficult, however, for people busy living and working in the modern world to take up this practice in the form it is typically presented, which is often too complicated and cumbersome for the modern man or woman to take up. For many, it is a challenge just to know where to start — a pain all too keenly felt by those who've tried to find time for prayer in the midst of the various needs of everyday life. Because of that difficulty, and even more importantly because of the immense importance of restoring the practice of sanctifying particular times of day, we put together this present volume that simplifies the ancient system of prayers, making it more accessible for daily practice, while preserving the essential structure and format of the prayer itself.

This simplified approach to the ancient prayer of the Church thus spans old and new, bringing a timeless Christian practice of the sacred into the midst of everyday life in the modern world. This simplified version even restores some of the more ancient elements that, although they have fallen out of memory in the West, are still in use by many churches in the East. This book of prayer, then, is intended to be truly Catholic in the sense that it is meant to be universal, taking into account the patterns of life of the modern world and bringing the ancient Christian inheritance to serve the needs of the present day in a way that speaks to a spirituality of sanctifying everyday life — a spirituality as old and as new as the Gospel itself. Thus, uniting elements of both East and West in the midst of an increasingly global and cosmopolitan society, it is our hope that the restoration of this ancient practice using the structure provided in this book will contribute to a renewal of orthodox Christian life in the midst of the world and the dynamic transformation of society.

May this prayer, a foretaste of your divine inheritance, enrich and transform you by the grace of almighty God, our loving Father, as you integrate this ancient and venerable practice into your daily life.

Over time, in the regular practice of these prayers, you will find yourself memorizing them as they permeate your heart. Thus learning these prayers by heart, they will be "a spiritual sacrifice pleasing to the Lord" and become, as it were, your own spontaneous prayers, forming in you the increasing ability to *pray unceasingly*.

I
RISING BEFORE DAWN

O Father of the World, Father of the ages, all creation serves you, and the entire universe, along with all the holy ones in the heavens offer praise before you.

Hymn (Early Christian Hymn, Egypt)
Tune: Ancient "Oxyrhynchus Hymn" Melody

Let the night be hushed | and grow silent,
Let the stars | dim their lights,
Let the rushing rivers | and the winds become calm.
And as we sing praise to | the Father, the Son and the Holy Spirit,
all the heavenly powers | echo back their praises:
"Amen! | Amen!"
Dominion always and praise, | and glory to God, the sole giver of good things.
Amen! | Amen!

II
MORNING PRAISES

+ God, come to my assistance;
Lord, make haste to help me.

Glory be to the Father, and to the Son,
and to the Holy Spirit,
as it was in the beginning, is now and always,
and unto the ages of ages. Amen. Alleluia!

Hymn *(Veni Creator Spiritus)*
Translated by A. Fortescue, adapted by C.M. Thompson

Come, Creator Spirit,
visit the the souls of your people,
fill with grace from on high,
the hearts which you have made.

You who are called the Advocate,
Gift of God most high,
living fount, fire, love,
and anointing of the spirit.

Sevenfold in your gifts,
Finger of the Father's right hand,
truly promised by the Father,
giving speech to our tongues.

Inflame our senses with you light,
pour love into our hearts,
and our weak bodies strengthen
with your lasting power.

Drive far away our enemy,
grant us peace in all times,
that led by you,
we may avoid all harm.

Through you may we know the Father,
and also know the Son,
and you, Spirit of them both,
May we believe for all time.

To God the Father be glory,
and to the Son, who rose from death,
and to the Advocate,
unto the ages of ages. Amen.

Psalm 1

Blessed is the man
who walks not in the counsel of the wicked,

nor stands in the path of sinners,
nor sits in the seat of scoffers.

but his delight is in the law of the Lord,
and on his law he meditates day and night.

He is like a tree planted by streams of flowing water,
who bears its fruit at the proper time,
and whose leaves never wither.

In all that he does, he prospers.
Not so the wicked, but they are like chaff that the
wind drives away.

Therefore the wicked will not stand in the judgment,
nor sinners in the gathering of the just;

for the Lord knows the way of the just,
but the way of the wicked will perish.

Glory be to the Father, and to the Son,
and to the Holy Spirit,
As it was in the beginning, is now and always,
and unto the ages of ages. Amen.

Short Reading *(Deut. 6:4-9)*

Hear, O Israel! The Lord, our God, is one Lord; and you shall love the Lord, your God, with all your heart, and with all your soul and with all your might. You shall take to heart the words which I enjoin on you today, and you shall teach them diligently to your children. You shall talk of them when you sit in your house and when you walk by the way, and when you lie down and when you rise. You shall bind them as a sign upon your hand and they shall be like frontlets before your eyes, and you shall write them on the doorposts of your house and on your gates.

Let us bless the Lord!

(Response) Thanks be to God!

Gospel Canticle *(Luke 1:68-79)*

+ Blessed be the Lord, the God of Israel,
for he has visited and redeemed his people.

And has raised up a horn of salvation for us
in the house of his servant David.

As he spoke through his holy prophets from of old
that we should be saved from our enemies
and from the hands of all who hate us.

To fulfill the mercy promised to our fathers
and to remember his holy covenant

The oath he swore to our father Abraham
that delivered from the hands of our enemies

We might serve him without fear,
holy and righteous before him all the days of our life.

You, my child, shall be called prophet of the Most High,
For you will go before the Lord to prepare his way

To give his people knowledge of salvation
by the forgiveness of their sins

Through the tender mercy of our God
when the day shall dawn upon us from on high

To give light to those who sit in darkness and the
shadow of death
To guide our feet into the way of peace.

Glory be to the Father, and to the Son,
and to the Holy Spirit,
As it was in the beginning, is now and always,
and unto the ages of ages. Amen.

Trisagion

Holy God, Holy Mighty One, Holy Immortal One,
have mercy on us.

Holy God, Holy Mighty One, Holy Immortal One,
have mercy on us.

Holy God, Holy Mighty One, Holy Immortal One,
have mercy on us.

Litany

For the peace from on high and the salvation of our souls, let us pray to the Lord.

(R) Lord, have mercy

For healthful seasons, abundance of the fruits of the earth, and peaceful times, let us pray to the Lord.

(R) Lord, have mercy

For this house and the whole region around us that the Lord will grant us mercy, peace, life, health, happiness, salvation, and the remission of our sins, let us pray to the Lord.

(R) Lord, have mercy

Lord, hear my prayer,
and let my cry come unto you.

The Lord's Prayer

Our Father, who art in heaven, hallowed be thy name. Thy kingdom come, thy will be done on earth as it is in heaven. Give us this day our daily bread, and forgive us our trespasses as we forgive those who trespass against us; and lead us not into temptation but deliver us from evil. For the kingdom, the power, and the glory are yours now and forever.

Closing Prayer

Let us pray.

May our actions, O Lord, begin with your inspiration and continue with your help, so that all our prayers and works may begin in you and through you reach completion through Christ our Lord. Amen.

+ May the Lord bless us, defend us from all evil, and bring us to everlasting life. Amen.

Let us bless the Lord.

(R) Thanks be to God!

III
MID-DAY PRAYER

+ God, come to my assistance;
Lord, make haste to help me.

Canticle *(Eph. 1:3-10)*

Blessed be the God and Father
of our Lord Jesus Christ

Who has blessed us in Christ
with every spiritual blessing in the heavens

Even as he chose us in him before the creation of the
world
That we should be holy and blameless before him.

He destined us in love to be his children through Jesus
Christ
according to the purpose of his will,

to the praise of his glorious grace
which he bestowed freely on us in the Beloved.

In him we have redemption through his blood,
the forgiveness of our trespasses,

in accordance with the riches of his grace
which he has lavished upon us.

For he has made known to us in all wisdom and insight
the mystery of his will

The purpose which he set forth in Christ for the
fulness of time,
To unite in him all things in heaven and on earth.

Glory be to the Father, and to the Son,
and to the Holy Spirit,
As it was in the beginning, is now and always,
and unto the ages of ages. Amen.

+ Let us bless the Lord!
Thanks be to God!

IV
EVENING SONG

+ God, come to my assistance;
Lord, make haste to help me.

Glory be to the Father, and to the Son,
and to the Holy Spirit,
as it was in the beginning, is now and always,
and unto the ages of ages. Amen. Alleluia!

Hymn *(Phos Hilaron)*
trans. by C.M.Thompson, 2014

O Joyous Light of the Holy Glory,
of the Immortal Father,
the heavenly, holy, O blessed, Jesus Christ.

As we approach the setting of the sun
and have seen the evening light
we sing praise to the one God: Father, Son, & Holy Spirit.

You are worthy
to be praised at all times
with holy and joyful voice.

O Son of God,
You are the Giver of Life,
and so the whole cosmos glorifies you.

Let my prayer arise before you like incense, O Lord
The lifting up of my hands like an evening oblation.

Psalm 116:12-19

How can I repay the Lord
for all his goodness to me?

The cup of salvation I will raise;
I will call upon the name of the Lord.

I will fulfill my vows to the Lord
before all his people

How precious in the eyes of the Lord
is the death of his holy ones.

Your servant, O Lord, your servant am I
the son of your handmaid;
you have loosed my bonds.

A thanksgiving sacrifice I make,
and will call upon the name of the Lord.

I will fulfill my vows to the Lord
before all his people,

in the courts of the house of the Lord,
in your midst, O Jerusalem.

Glory be to the Father, and to the Son,
and to the Holy Spirit,
As it was in the beginning, is now and always,
and unto the ages of ages. Amen.

Short Reading *(I Peter 3:10-11)*

You who would love life and see good days – keep your tongue from evil and your lips that they speak no deceit; turn away from evil and do good; seek after peace and pursue it.

Let us bless the Lord!

> **(R)** Thanks be to God!

Gospel Canticle *(Luke 1:46-55)*

+ My soul magnifies the Lord
and my spirit rejoices in God my savior,
for he has looked on the humility of his servant.

Behold, henceforth all generations will call me blessed,
for the mighty one has done great things for me
and holy is his name.

His mercy is on those who fear him
from generation to generation.

He has shown the strength of his arm
and scattered the proud in the imagination of their hearts,

He has put down the powerful from their thrones,
and has exalted the humble.

He has filled the hungry with good things,
and the rich he has sent away empty.

He has helped his servant Israel,
In remembrance of his mercy

As he spoke to our fathers
to Abraham and his descendants forever.

Glory be to the Father, and to the Son,
and to the Holy Spirit,
As it was in the beginning, is now and always,
and unto the ages of ages. Amen.

Trisagion

Holy God, Holy Mighty One, Holy Immortal One,
have mercy on us.

Holy God, Holy Mighty One, Holy Immortal One,
have mercy on us.

Holy God, Holy Mighty One, Holy Immortal One,
have mercy on us.

For the remission of our sins, and for peace and freedom for all peoples throughout the world that we may all live in unity, peace, and concord, let us pray to the Lord.

(R) Lord, have mercy

That He will bestow on us an increase of grace and wisdom, of mutual trust and confidence, of perseverance in every good work, and of spiritual growth and maturity, let us pray to the Lord.

(R) Lord, have mercy

Remember, O Lord, the coming down of the rains, and the waters, and the rivers, and bless them that they may bring life and abundance, we beseech you to hear us, O Lord.

(R) Lord, have mercy

Grant eternal life and peace to all the faithful departed who have gone from among us, we beseech you to hear us, O Lord.

(R) Lord, have mercy

Lord, hear my prayer,
and let my cry come unto you.

The Lord's Prayer

Our Father, who art in heaven, hallowed be thy name. Thy kingdom come, thy will be done on earth as it is in heaven. Give us this day our daily bread, and forgive us our trespasses as we forgive those who trespass against us; and lead us not into temptation but deliver us from evil.

Closing Prayer

May this evening offering of our service magnify you, O Lord, for, as you looked upon the humility of the Virgin Mary for our salvation, so make us worthy to be exalted to the fullness of redemption through our Lord Jesus Christ, your Son, who lives and reigns with you in the Holy Spirit, one God unto the ages of ages. Amen.

✝ May the Lord bless us, defend us from all evil, and bring us to everlasting life. Amen.

Let us bless the Lord.

> (R) Thanks be to God!

V
COMPLETION OF DAY AT NIGHTFALL

✝ God, come to my assistance;
Lord, make haste to help me.

Glory be to the Father, and to the Son,
and to the Holy Spirit,
as it was in the beginning, is now and always,
and unto the ages of ages. Amen. Alleluia!

Forgiveness Rite (when praying in community)

(Together) I confess to almighty God and to you, my **brother/sister/brothers/sisters**, that I have greatly sinned, in my thoughts and in my words, in what I have done, and in what I have failed to do, through my fault, through my fault, through my most grievous fault. Therefor, I ask the Blessed Mary ever Virgin, all the angels and saints, and you my **brother/sister/brothers/sisters**, to pray for me to the Lord, our God.

(Together) May almighty God have mercy on you, forgive you your sins, and bring you to everlasting life. Amen.

Prayer for God's Mercy and Blessing

Kyrie Eleison.
Christe Eleison.
Kyrie Eleison

Hymn *(Te Lucis Ante Terminum)*

To you, before the end of light,
Creator of all things, we pray,
That in your loving kindness might,
Protect and guard us through the night

In you may our hearts dream this night
In you may they find restful sleep,
And always with the coming light,
Together sing your glorious might.

Health-giving life, grant us, we pray,
The heat of life in us renew,
And drive the fog of night away
With the clear brightness of your light.

Cast far from us all dreams that fright,
And all the phantoms of the night
And bind our deadly enemy
That free from stain we all may be.

Grant this, Father Almighty,
Through Jesus Christ, our God and Lord,
Who with you reigns continually,
With Holy Spirit, thrice-adored.

Psalm 91

He who dwells in the shelter of the Most High,
and abides in the shadow of the Almighty,

Will say to the Lord, "my refuge and my stronghold;
my God, in whom I trust."

He will deliver you from the snare of the fowler,
and from the deadly pestilence;

he will cover you with his pinions
and under his wings you will find refuge;
his faithfulness is buckler and shield.

You will not fear the terror of the night,
nor the arrow that flies by day,

Nor the busyness that prowls in the darkness,
nor the destruction that lays waste at noon.

A thousand may fall at your side,
ten thousand fall at your right;
but you it will never approach.

Your eyes have only to look
to see how the wicked are repaid.

Because you have taken refuge in the Lord,
and made the Most High your dwelling,

No evil shall befall you,
no scourge come near your tent.

For he will command his angels over you
to guard you in all your ways.

On their hands they will bear you up,
lest you dash your foot against a stone.

You will tread on the lion and the dragon,
the young lion and the serpent you will trample.

Because he cleaves to me in love, I will deliver him;
I will protect him for he knows my name.

When he calls I will answer; I will be with him in trouble,
I will rescue him and glorify him.

With length of days I will fill him,
and show him my salvation.

Glory be to the Father, and to the Son,
and to the Holy Spirit,
As it was in the beginning, is now and always,
and unto the ages of ages. Amen.

They shall see the Lord face to face, and bear his name on their foreheads. The night shall be no more; they will need no light from lamps or the sun, for the Lord God will be their light, and they shall reign for ages of ages.

Let us bless the Lord!

> **(R)** Thanks be to God!

Antiphon

Protect us Lord, as we stay awake; watch over us as we sleep, that awake we may keep watch with Christ, and asleep rest in his peace.

Gospel Canticle

+ Lord, now let your servant go in peace,
according to your word;

for my eyes have seen your salvation
which who have prepared in the presence of all peoples,

a light for revelation to the Gentiles,
and the glory of your people Israel.

Glory be to the Father, and to the Son,
and to the Holy Spirit,
As it was in the beginning, is now and always,
and unto the ages of ages. Amen.

Antiphon

Protect us Lord, as we stay awake; watch over us as we sleep, that awake we may keep watch with Christ, and asleep rest in his peace.

Closing Prayer

Visit this house, we beg you, O Lord, and drive far from it all the deadly power of the enemy. May your holy angels dwell here to keep us in peace, and may your blessing be upon us always, through Christ our Lord. Amen.

+ May the all powerful Lord grant us a quiet night and a perfect end. Amen.

Final Hymn

Hail Mary, full of grace, the Lord is with you. Blessed are you among women, and blessed is the fruit of your womb, Jesus. Holy Mary, mother of God, pray for us sinners now and at the hour of our death. Amen.

(It is custom for the head of the family to bless each member of the household with holy water at this time. If praying on your own, make the sign of the cross with holy water)

VI
GOING TO BED

Gospel Reading *(John 1:1-19)*

In the beginning was the Word, and the Word was with God, and the Word was God. He was in the beginning with God; all things were made through him, and without him was not anything made that was made. In him was life, and the life was the light of men. The light shines in the darkness, and the darkness has not overcome it.

There was a man sent from God, whose name was John. He came for testimony, to bear witness to the light, that all might believe through him. He was not the light, but came to bear witness to the light.

The true light that enlightens every man was coming into the world. He was in the world, and the world was made through him, yet the world knew him not. He came to his own home, and his own people received him not. But to all who received him, who believed in his name, he gave power to become children of God; who were born, not of blood nor of the will of the flesh nor of the will of men, but of God.

And the Word became flesh and dwelt among us, full of grace and truth; we have beheld his glory, glory as of the only Son from the Father. (John bore witness to him, and cried, "This is he of whom I said, `He who comes after me ranks before me, for before me he was'"). And from his fulness have we all received, grace upon grace. For the law was given through Moses; grace and truth came to be through Jesus Christ. No one has ever seen God; the only Son, who is in the bosom of the Father, he has made him known.

Closing

Into your hands, Lord, I commend my spirit.

Let us bless the Lord!

> **(R)** Thanks be to God!

VII
PSALM FOR MIDNIGHT

✝ God, come to my assistance;
Lord, make haste to help me.

Psalm 134

Come, bless the Lord,
all you servants of the Lord,
who stand by night in the house of the Lord.

Lift up your hands to the holy place,
and bless the Lord.

May the Lord bless you from Zion,
He who made heaven and earth.

Glory be to the Father, and to the Son,
and to the Holy Spirit,
As it was in the beginning, is now and always,
and unto the ages of ages. Amen.

✝ Let us bless the Lord!

(R) Thanks be to God!

PRAYERS

FOR

VARIOUS OCCASIONS

SONG OF GRATITUDE

For Giving Thanks

Te Deum, trans. & arr. by Cameron M. Thompson
Tune: "Thaxted"

O God, we laud and praise you! Confessing you are Lord!
You, the Eternal Father, by all the world adored:
To you do all the angels, all Powers of the heavens,
The Cherubim and Seraphim unceasingly proclaim,
Crying, Holy Holy Holy, Lord God of Sabaöth,
Plenteous-full the heavens and the earth, by your glorious
majesty!

The Apostles' glorious choir, the prophets' number praised,
The Martyrs' white-robed army, praise you through all their days.
Throughout all lands of the Earth, you the holy Church
proclaims,
Father, great in majesty, your true and only Son,
Holy, with the Spirit Paraclete, be worshiped and adored,
Christ, the Father's eternal Son, King of Glory and our Lord!

Liberating us you became man, not scorning Virgin's womb,
You, by conquering the sting of death, for all believers
op'ed the heav'ns.
You are seated at God's right-hand, in the Father's glory,
We believe you come as Judge, therefor we beseech you,
Help your servants whom you have redeemed by your
most precious blood,
Make us numbered with your holy ones in Eternal Glory!

Make your people safe, O Lord, bless Your inheritance,
And govern them and uphold them unto eternity.
Each day we bless you, and through the ages praise Your Name.
Deign, O Lord, this very day, to keep us without sin,
Have mercy on us, O Lord, be your mercy over us.
As, we've hoped in You—O Lord, we've hoped!—may
we ne'er be overcome!

PSALM OF REPENTANCE (50/51)

To Prepare for Confession and Communion

Have mercy on me, O God,
according to your great mercy;
according to the multitude of your compassion
blot out my transgressions.

Wash me thoroughly from my iniquity,
and cleanse me from my sin!
For I know my transgressions,
and my sin is ever before me.

Against you alone have I sinned,
and what is evil in your sight I have done,
and so you are justified in your sentence
and blameless in your judgment.

Behold, I was conceived in iniquity,
and a sinner when my mother brought me forth.
Behold, you have loved truth;
You have made known to me the secrets of your wisdom.

Sprinkle me with hyssop, and I shall be made clean;
wash me, and I shall be whiter than snow.

Make me hear joy and gladness;
That the bones you have crushed may rejoice.
Turn away your face from my sins,
and blot out all my iniquities.

Create in me a clean heart, O God,
and renew a steadfast spirit within me.
Cast me not away from your presence,
and take not your Holy Spirit from me.

Restore to me the joy of your salvation,
and uphold me with a willing spirit.
Then I will teach transgressors your ways,
and sinners will return to you.

Deliver me from bloodguilt, O God,
the God of my salvation,
and my tongue will praise your justice.
O Lord, open my lips,
and my mouth shall declare your praise.

For you have no delight in sacrifice;
were I to give a burnt offering, you would not be pleased.
The sacrifice to God is a broken spirit;
a heart contrite and humble, O God, you will not despise.

Do good to Zion in your good pleasure;
that the walls of Jerusalem may be rebuilt,
then you shall be pleased with right sacrifice,
with oblations and whole burnt offerings;
then shall bulls be offered on your altar.

Glory be to the Father, and to the Son,
And to the Holy Spirit.
As it was in the beginning, is now and always,
And unto the ages of ages. Amen.

LITANY OF SUPPLICATION

In Times of Distress, Tribulation, or any Great Need

God the Father,
  Have mercy on us.
God the Son,
  Have mercy on us.
God the Holy Spirit,
  Have mercy on us.
O holy, blessed, and glorious Trinity, one God;
  Have mercy on us.

Remember not, O Lord, our offenses, nor the offenses of
our forefathers; neither take vengeance for our sins: Spare
us, good Lord, spare your people, whom you have
redeemed with your most precious blood, and in your
mercy keep us for ever.

O Lord, arise and help us;
  And deliver us for the sake of your name.

O God, we have heard with our ears, and our fathers have
declared unto us, the noble works that you did in their
days, and in the ancient days before them.
  O Lord, arise and help us; deliver us for the sake of your name.

Glory be to the Father, and to the Son,
and to the Holy Spirit;
as it was in the beginning, is now and always,
and unto the ages of ages. Amen.
  O Lord, arise and help us; deliver us for the sake of your name.

From our enemies defend us, O Christ;
Graciously behold our afflictions
With pity behold the sorrows of our hearts;
Mercifully forgive the sins of your people.
Favorably with mercy hear our prayers;
O Son of David, have mercy on us.
Both now and forever vouchsafe to hear us, O Lord;
Graciously hear us, O Christ; hear and answer us, O Lord Jesus Christ

Son of God, we beseech you to hear us.
Son of God, we beseech you to hear us.
O Lamb of God, who take away the sins of the world;
Grant us your peace.
O Lamb of God, who take away the sins of the world;
Have mercy on us.
O Christ, hear us.
O Christ, hear us.

Kyrie Eleison.
Kyrie Eleison.
Christe Eleison.
Christe Eleison.
Kyrie Eleison.
Kyrie Eleison.

Our Father, who art in heaven, hallowed be thy name. Thy kingdom come. Thy will be done, on earth as it is in heaven. Give us this day our daily bread. And forgive us our trespasses as we forgive those who trespass against us. And lead us not into temptation, but deliver us from evil. Amen.

From our enemies defend us, O Lord.
Graciously look upon our afflictions.
With pity behold the sorrows of our hearts.
Mercifully forgive the sins of your people.
Favorably with mercy hear our prayers.
O Son of David, have mercy on us.
Both now and ever vouchsafe to hear us, O Lord.
Graciously hear us, O Christ; Graciously hear us, O Lord Jesus Christ.

O Lord, let your mercy shine upon us;
As we place all our trust in you.

Let us pray.
We humbly beseech you, O Father, mercifully to look upon our infirmities; and, for the glory of you name, turn from us all those evils that we justly have deserved; and grant, that in all our troubles we may put our whole trust and confidence in your mercy, and for evermore serve you in holiness and purity of living, for your honor and glory; through your only-begotten son, our Lord Jesus Christ.
Amen.

PRAYER FOR THE DECEASED

May the angels lead you into paradise;
may the martyrs greet you at your arrival
and lead you into the holy City of Jerusalem.
May the choir of Angels greet you
and like Lazarus, who once was a poor man,
may you have eternal rest.

O God of spirits and of all flesh, Who has trampled down death and overthrown the devil, and given life to your world, O Lord, give rest to the souls of your departed servants in a place of brightness, a place of refreshment, a place of repose, where all sickness, sighing, and sorrow have fled away. Pardon every transgression which they have committed, whether by word or deed or thought. For you are the all-good God who loves mankind; because there is no man who lives yet does not sin, for you only are without sin, your righteousness is for all eternity, and your word is truth.

For you are the Resurrection, the Life, and the Repose of your servants who have fallen asleep, O Christ our God, and unto you we ascribe glory, together with your Father, who is from everlasting, and your all-holy, good, and life-creating Spirit, now and forever unto the ages of ages. Amen.

Eternal rest grant unto him/her/them O Lord.
And let perpetual light shine upon him/her/them.
May they Rest In Peace.

PRAYER OF THE HEART

In between the hours for prayer, you can continue to cultivate prayer in the heart and pray unceasingly, by keeping constant wakefulness over your heart (*nepsis/ eyerutho*), continually invoking the healing and sanctifying name of our Lord Jesus Christ in the ancient and time-honored short prayer known as the Jesus Prayer.

> "Lord Jesus Christ, Son of God,
> have mercy on me, a sinner."

PRAYER OF FORGIVENESS

O Lord of all creation, I hereby forgive whoever has hurt me or done me any wrong; whether intentionally or unintentionally; whether by word or by deed; whether against my body, my belongings, my dignity, or anything else I have; whether in the present, the past, or the future; no matter who they are. May no person in the world be punished because of me. Amen.

THE TOOLS FOR LIVING WELL

from
Saint Benedict of Nursia

In the first place to love the Lord your God with all your heart, all your soul, and all your strength. Then, your neighbor as yourself.

Then, to not kill, to not commit adultery, to not steal, to not desire to possess something that you do not have.

To not give false testimony, to honor all men and women, and to not do to another what you would not have done to yourself, and to turn away from yourself in order to follow Christ.

To keep your body in check, not seeking after pleasures.

To love fasting, to restore the poor to good condition, to clothe the naked, to visit the sick, to bury the dead.

To help those in trouble, to console the sorrowing, to keep yourself a stranger to the ways of this passing age, and to prefer nothing to the love of Christ.

To not give way to wrath, to not hold a grudge, to not hold deceit in your heart, to not make a false peace, to not neglect charity.

To not swear an oath, lest you commit perjury, but to speak the truth with both heart and tongue.

To not return evil for evil, to do no harm but even bear patiently the harm done to you.

To love your enemies, to not curse those who curse you, but rather to bless them, and to bear persecution for the sake of justice.

To not be proud, nor an alcoholic, nor an over-eater.

To not be sleepy, to not be lazy, to not be a grumbler, to not be a detractor.

To put your trust in God, to attribute to God, rather than to yourself, the good you see in yourself, but to recognize that any evil is your own doing and take responsibility for it.

To hold in fear and awe the day of judgment, to dread Gehenna, to desire eternal life with all the longing of your spirit.

To keep death daily before your eyes, to keep watch at all times over the actions of your life, to know for certain that God gazes upon you in every place.

To dash at once against Christ the evil thoughts that come into your heart, and to disclose them to your spiritual advisor.

To keep your tongue from wicked and perverse speech, to not love a lot of speaking, to not utter empty words or those fit for laughter, nor to love excessive or boisterous laughter.

To listen eagerly to the holy readings, to lean frequently on prayer.

To confess your past sins with sighs and tears daily to God in prayer, and to correct them for the future.

To not carry out the desires of the flesh, and to be averse to your own whims.

To obey the orders of the legitimate authority in all things, even though they themselves might act otherwise, mindful of the Lord's admonition: "What they say, do ye; but what they do, do ye not."

To not desire to be called holy before you really are; but to actually be holy first, so that you can truly be called holy.

To fulfill the commandments of God in your daily action, to love chastity, to hate no one, to not have jealousy, to not exercise envy, to not love contention, and to flee from flattery.

To honor your elders and to love your juniors.

To pray for your enemies in the love of Christ, to make peace with someone whom you've quarreled with before the setting of the sun, and to never despair of the mercy of God.

Behold, these are the tools of the craft of the spirit, which, if they have been applied unceasingly day and night, and are returned to the Master on judgment day, will merit for us from the Lord the reward he promised: "Which eye has not seen, nor the ear heard, what God has prepared for those who love Him."